HOW TO HAVE

HIGH

DOLLAR

GARAGE

ALE

Jean Hines

VISTA MARK PUBLICATIONS

Copyright © 1989 by Jean L. Hines

Published by Vista Mark Publications
Printed in the United States of America

ISBN 0-9622425-4-3

CONTENTS

Introduction

1 Decisions To Make   7
    Timing
    Other People's Items
    Your Choices

2 Attitudes Are Catching   12

3 Family Involvement   14
    Ways To Get Family
        Interest
    Getting Started
    Family Benefits
    Individual Benefits
    Areas Of Family
        Participation
    Young Entrepreneurs

4 Developing A Buy Atmosphere   19
    Classified Ads
    Road Signs
    Store Posters
    Garage Layout
    Personal Contact
    Salesmanship

5 Nitty Gritty   28
    Comfort
    Secrets Of Pricing
    Organization
    Secrets Of Display

6 Being Prepared   35
        Quick, Easy Recipes
        Children's Activities
        Weather
        Record Keeping
        Change
        Early Start

7 Safeguards   51

8 Real Treasure   53
        Treasure Hinting
        Buyers
        Sources Of Information
        Old Treasure
        Future Treasure

9 Helpful Hints   60

10 Checklist For Success   68

11 Next Time   73

        Index   75

GARAGE SALES ARE ...

... **Lots of fun** or an emotional drain,

... **Exciting** or boring,

... **Smooth running** or a hassle,

... **Something you will look forward to doing again and again** or something you would never do again if your life depended on it,

... **Very profitable** or hardly worth the effort.

A BIG DOLLAR SALE DONE WITH EASE happens with knowledge and preparation.

. KNOWLEDGE of
    WHAT to do
    HOW to do it
    WHEN to do it

. PREPARATION by
    DOING what you know to do in a timely manner

With this complete guide, you are ready to have a VERY PROFITABLE, SMOOTH RUNNING, EXCITING GARAGE SALE each and every time.

DECISIONS

TO MAKE

TIMING

SPRING, SUMMER, FALL

SPRINGTIME is an ideal time for a garage sale. You have had all winter to clean closets and gather items you no longer want. Other people have been inside all winter and are EAGER TO BE OUT. They are also READY TO BUY.

SUMMER can be quite hot, and enthusiasm for going to sales slows somewhat.

By FALL many people have what I term "Garage Sale Fatigue" and become more picky in what they buy.

Be assured, however, that you can have a VERY PROFITABLE SALE whatever time of year you choose. With so many people in our country and so many varied schedules, there are often people who do not have a chance to go to garage sales until late summer or fall. Thus, fresh enthusiastic buyers are constantly looking for sales.

YOUR SCHEDULE
Consult your calendar for upcoming activities. You will want to have your garage sale when no other time consuming events are scheduled. Some examples are: getting ready to leave on vacation, or planning for a visit from family or friends from out of town. This may seem silly to mention; but with our busy lives, it is not always easy to find available time for a sale. IT IS, HOWEVER, ALWAYS POSSIBLE.

CONSIDER WHEN PEOPLE GET PAID
If convenient, schedule your sale on the weekend that people get paid. They will naturally have more dollars available to buy your items and will feel freer to do so.

HOLIDAYS
Avoid holidays. People will be spending money other ways at that time.

SCHOOL
Right before school people spend their money for items necessary for school. If you have some top quality clothes that would be good to wear for starting to school, this might be an exceptional time for a sale. Otherwise, a sale at this time is usually not very profitable.

NUMBER OF DAYS
The usual choices are from 1 to 3 days (Thur, Fri, Sat.). If you work outside the home, you might want to be open Saturday only unless family or friends can help other days. Many people think 2 days are enough; but as long as you have done all the work of getting ready, adding a 3rd day is no chore. A 3 day sale is the most profitable.

Check several different weeks of local newspaper ads to see what days are most prevalent in your area. For the best results have your sale on these days.

HOURS
Following are some areas of choice:
HOW EARLY TO OPEN THE SALE
No matter what time you choose, there will probably be "early birds" eagerly waiting for your opening on the first day. (Time Choices: 7,8,9)

HOW LATE TO STAY OPEN IN THE EVENING (Choices: 5 till dark). Look in the classifieds to see what is normal in your area, but be free to choose the closing time best suited to your schedule. A few extra dollars can be made by being open for evening shoppers.

SATURDAY?
If this is a 2 or 3 day sale, you will probably want shorter hours on Saturday (perhaps closing at noon). If this is the only day for the sale, longer hours are desirable.

INCLUDING OTHER PEOPLE'S ITEMS

There are times and situations when you will prefer to have only your own things in a sale. Usually, however, you will want to have friends, family and neighbors include items. It can be very helpful, a lot more fun, and **definitely more profitable with others involved.**

BENEFITS OF HAVING OTHERS:
. A larger number of items to list in the newspaper ad for drawing buyers.
. With more buyers attending, you will sell more of your items
. Help with setting up and organizing.
. Help with the sale (this can give you free time for running to the grocery, starting the evening meal, answering the phone when there are customers).
. More enjoyment having someone to talk with when there is a time-break between customers.

DECIDE ON THE BEST DATES FOR YOU then invite others to participate.

Trying to get everyone's schedules to coincide is very difficult. There will always be someone who can't participate on the dates chosen. So, unless it is easy to change and find other dates agreeable to all, don't feel badly following your original plans. Others will understand.

There will always be more garage sales. In fact, the person unable to participate in your sale might decide to have one later. She will, no doubt, be delighted for you to include some of your unsold items.

YOUR CHOICES:

DATES OF SALE _____

DAYS _____

1ST DAY HOURS _____

2ND DAY HOURS_____

SATURDAY HOURS_____

WHO TO ASK _____

_____

_____

_____

_____

ATTITUDES ARE CATCHING

Your attitude in preparing for a garage sale will in a large part determine what kind of cooperation will be received from the family.

Knowing WHAT to do, WHEN to do it, and HOW to make a garage sale easy, will enable you to have a calm, positive, expectant attitude, and the family will too.

If you have children, make this a fun time and learning experience. Get them involved. See the chapter on "Family Involvement".

Everyone loves to get a good bargain. In fact, people often appreciate and take better care of a good bargain than something given to them free.

Rather than viewing garage sale items as junk you want to be rid of, consider them as real bargains to bring delight to someone else. Then, when you sell something, you get a triple thrill.

. Your house is less cluttered.

. Another person is pleased.

. You are excited about the money in your pocket for something you did not want anymore.

FAMILY INVOLVEMENT

It is important to have the family's cooperation whether or not they get involved. In other words, if they are not going to help, at least, they won't hinder. It is desirable, of course, if the family will participate in a positive way.

WAYS TO GET THE FAMILY INTERESTED

The best way to get everyone interested is to help them see HOW IT WILL BENEFIT THEM individually or as a group.

GETTING STARTED

Begin by talking about the garage sale. Say "**WE'RE** GOING TO HAVE A GARAGE SALE." Notice the "We're" is not an "I'm". If you start by saying "I'm", you can be sure that it will be ALL YOURS. Remember your attitude will make a big difference in getting the family interested. Be excited, positive, and enthusiastic with the announcement.

FAMILY BENEFITS

If there is something the family has been wanting (TV, VCR), or someplace EVERYONE has been wanting to go (amusement park, vacation), BE TALKING ABOUT IT in connection with the garage sale.

Call a family meeting for their input. This is an excellent opportunity for training in goal setting and team effort in accomplishing it. Again remember your attitude makes a difference.

Success of this approach depends on....
. Members of family being interested.
. Group commitment to help.
. Group follow through.

It is not always easy to go this way, but it can be very rewarding and lots of fun.

Since you know your family, you can decide if this might work well.

INDIVIDUAL BENEFITS

Even more powerful than family benefit is individual benefit.

CHILDREN OF ALL AGES will get excited about selling some of their things to get money. Let them have the money from their items. It will be surprising what they will be willing to sell. You will probably want to keep a close check on what is brought out for the sale.

Note: With younger children you might want to limit their money making to be from toys and games only. Keep clothing money separate since clothes have to be replaced.

With older children if they have bought the clothes, let them have the money from clothes as well as other items.

YOUNGER CHILDREN get excited with something different going on. This might be enough to gain their interest and cooperation. Let them help. Young children are always eager to help do grown up things. There will be lots of little chores they can do.

HUSBANDS often are happy to cooperate if they know old unwanted items can be turned into cash. This is a good opportunity for him (or you, if he agrees) to go through his clothes, tools, etc. and get rid of items not used. Some men get quite involved in garage sales, most do not. So don't be disappointed if he is not very interested. Be thrilled if he will help.

AREAS OF FAMILY PARTICIPATION

CLEANING THE GARAGE - After hosing the garage, the kids can run through the sprinkler.

SETTING UP - tables, clothesline, etc.).

MAKING SIGNS - These can be exciting and fun for the children.

MEALS (making, cooking, serving) - This can be a good learning experience. Older children might even assume the planning and preparing of a meal. Everyone can help with setting the table, serving and clean up.

TENDING THE SALE

. Watching to let you know when someone is coming if you are in the house.

. Sitting outside to handle everything.

This is wonderful experience for children.

Take time to teach them

. How to greet people (important people skill to develop).

. What to do if someone has a question.

. How to count money.

. How to keep sales records.

CARRYING THINGS in and out of garage morning and evening.

RUNNING ERRANDS to the store and at home. (There will be lots of errands in preparing for the sale).

PRICING - you will probably want to do this mostly yourself (including helping the children mark a fair price on their items).

COUNTING THE MONEY - Everyone likes to count to see how much they have made.

If you are wanting to keep most of the garage sale money for yourself that is ok. You will probably be doing most of the work. Your money no doubt gets absorbed into the family budget most of the time, but if you are wanting something special for yourself, go for it.

YOUNG ENTREPRENEURS

Recently I heard of a lady whose children sold hot dogs and soda pop at their garage sale. It was an area sale day so there were many sales in the allotment and an enormous number of people.

Even if yours is the only sale in the area, your children might enjoy setting up a lemonade stand (if the weather is hot) or selling coffee (if the weather is a little nippy).

Use your wise judgement and make it fun so the children will enjoy it no matter how much they sell.

DEVELOPING

A BUY

ATMOSPHERE

How customers perceive the sale from START TO FINISH is very important. It helps determine HOW MUCH THEY WILL BUY and WHAT THEY WILL BE WILLING TO PAY for the items.

ADVERTISEMENTS

The first contact people will have with the sale is through your advertising, either a CLASSIFIED AD in the newspaper, a SIGN by the road, or a POSTER at the grocery store.

CLASSIFIED ADS

Classified ads are relatively inexpensive and an

absolute must. For cost sake you will want ads to be SHORT, and for effect sake you will want them to be SMART.

An ad should first GET PEOPLE'S ATTENTION (stand out from other ads). Second, an ad should ATTRACT THE READERS (make them want to be certain to come to your sale, even if it is a little out of the way).

. USE ABBREVIATIONS WHEREVER POSSIBLE. Some papers charge by the line.
. USE ADJECTIVES - LIKE: Huge, Giant, Multi Family, 5 Family. These show a larger choice of items.
. LIST INDIVIDUAL ITEMS you feel would help attract people - mower, trundle bed, air conditioner, baby clothes, TV, bike, antiques, etc. When people come for a specific item they will usually browse and often buy something, even if it is not the item they specifically came to see.
. ALWAYS ADD the words "lots of misc. items". This builds curiosity. No one wants to miss out on a large selection of good deals.
. REMEMBER TO PUT IN THE DAYS
. REMEMBER TO PUT IN THE TIMES
. REMEMBER TO PUT IN THE LOCATION
    I have seen ads with some of these 3 basic essentials missing. No doubt the people having the sale were quite disappointed with the turn out.

    If your house is hard to find, give specific directions. The little bit of extra ad cost will more than pay for itself. People won't hunt long for a sale they aren't finding.

A CAUTION IS NEEDED - BE FACTUAL.

If you don't have lots, don't say you do. If you don't have a huge sale, don't say so. If a mower is sold before the sale, don't put it in the ad. All these things antagonize and disappoint customers. It is possible, if the sale appears not to be what was advertised, that people will glance from the car and leave without looking at anything.

SAMPLE OF WINNING AD:

> **5 FAMILY SALE** 2340 Profit St. (off Stoneyridge Blvd.) Mower, weights, TV, crib, chair, boat, toys, comics, many clothes esp. boys, lots of misc. Thur.Fri. 8-6 Sat. 9-12.

ROAD SIGNS

Signs are the next biggest attention getter. They don't have to be professional, but it is important that they are NEAT, VISIBLE, AND EYE CATCHING.

The NEWSPAPER often gives several free SIGNS when you place your ad. These signs are fine but too small to be seen well from a passing car. Use these at the stores and in front of your house.

White CARDBOARD is an excellent choice for making signs. The lettering stands out on white. When using cardboard, fasten it securely to a 3-4 foot stake so it will withstand rain and wind. The side of a cardboard BOX can also be used effectively and requires little anchoring.

LETTERING THE SIGN:
. USE A YARDSTICK to mark a top and bottom line for each row of letters so LETTERS are the same height.
. PENCIL IN where letters are to go so they can be well spaced.
. USE MAGIC MARKERS or regular PAINT to do the lettering.
. USE COLORS that will STAND OUT.
. BE CREATIVE.

CONTENTS:
. USE CAPITAL LETTERS 4 or more inches high.
. USE ARROWS to point direction or give address (arrows are very effective).

PLACEMENT:
. PLACE SIGNS WHERE THEY ARE EASY TO SEE
. AT ALL MAIN ROADS leading to your house.
. AT THE END OF YOUR STREET IN FRONT OF YOUR HOUSE.
. TAKE SIGNS DOWN AFTER THE SALE.

SOME CHILDREN CAN MAKE EXCELLENT SIGNS. They can be quite creative in making them eye-catching. Be sure to give instruction on layout along with directions on how to use the yardstick to get all the lettering the same size and centered.

STORE POSTERS

Posters are helpful but not critical. The newspaper ad and road signs are the "biggies".

A couple things to think about with posters:

. BE SURE THEY ARE NEAT.
. LETTERING SHOULD BE BIG ENOUGH TO BE READ FROM A DISTANCE.
. INCLUDE ESSENTIALS LIKE: 4 FAMILY GARAGE SALE, DAYS, TIMES, LOCATION. Draw a small map if it would be helpful.
. MEDIUM SIZE - STORES DON'T LIKE A LOT OF CLUTTER - maximum of 10" x 14".
. GET STORE'S PERMISSION TO PUT POSTER UP.
. BE SURE TO GO BACK AND TAKE IT DOWN.

GENERAL LAYOUT OF GARAGE

Remember we are still talking about DEVELOPING A POSITIVE BUY ATTITUDE in customers, so they WILL BUY and WILL GLADLY **PAY TOP DOLLAR**.

NEATNESS COUNTS - Counts up to bigger profits.

. SWEEP OR HOSE THE GARAGE FLOOR.
. STRAIGHTEN VISIBLE ITEMS IN GARAGE.

. COVER ITEMS YOU DO NOT WANT SEEN. Old sheets or table cloths are good for hiding MESSY AREAS, AND VALUABLE ITEMS.

. DUST OR WIPE OFF tables or boards used to display items. Cover with something if they look unappealing.

. CLEAN & FRESHEN ITEMS TO BE SOLD
> WASH DISHES & CLOTHES, if soiled.
> WASH OR WIPE OTHER ITEMS.
> FRESHEN CLOTHES - If they are wrinkled, put a few at a time in a dryer with a damp towel for a quick spruce up.

. PLAN TO FOLD AND HANG UP SALE ITEMS.

Doing all of the above might seem time consuming, but it really takes just a LITTLE BIT MORE EFFORT. The rewards are WELL WORTH IT. People will pay TWO or THREE TIMES MORE than they would pay otherwise.

When it is noticeable that you value your items, others will too.

PERSONAL CONTACT

This is a very important area. When people feel WELCOME and AT EASE, they will be better able to think about the items for sale.

Along with hunting for outstanding deals, some people go to garage sales because they are lonely or bored. So it is helpful when it is a FRIENDLY PLEASANT EXPERI-ENCE.

. WITH A SMILE SAY "HI" TO EVERYONE.
. START A CONVERSATION. You will know whether someone wants to talk more or not.
. BE AVAILABLE.
    . IF YOU STEP INTO THE HOUSE for a minute, keep an open ear and eye. Greeting people as they arrive is important. Some people feel they are intruding if there is no one there.
    . WHEN FRIENDS ARE HELPING, give PRIORITY ATTENTION TO THE CUSTOMER. Greet people immediately and be available to answer questions. You can always re-sume a conversation with a friend. When ignored, people think they are imposing and won't feel free to buy. Be sensitive. After an initial greeting some people would rather be left alone. Be sure you are QUICK TO BE AVAILABLE if they do desire your help.

REMEMBER your 1st goal is to make people feel wel-come (this is your home). The 2nd goal is to make the atmosphere the most favorable possible for them to want to buy.

SALESMANSHIP

Your whole purpose for having a sale is to make money

on items you no long need or want. To make the MOST PROFIT POSSIBLE, a little salesmanship helps.

At garage sales salesmanship is merely giving a little bit of added attention. This is all done in a very LOW GEAR and CASUAL MANNER.

SECRET: BE IN TUNE WITH YOUR CUSTOMERS AND THEIR NEEDS.

. WHEN YOU SEE SOMEONE SHOWING INTEREST IN SOMETHING - talk with them about it IF they are receptive.
. LOOKING THROUGH CLOTHES - FIND OUT WHAT THEIR NEEDS ARE. Ask "What sizes are you looking for?" You know what is available. Help them find the size. If there is nothing in that size, OFFER THEM AN ALTERNATIVE: For growing children a next size larger is often desirable.
. DRAPERIES, SHEETS, TABLE CLOTHS - Offer size information. Get a yardstick or tape measure for them.
. TV OR STEREO, ETC. - Turn it on. Let them operate it.
. MUSICAL INSTRUMENT - Offer to let them handle it or play it.
. BIKES, APPLIANCES, MOWERS, ETC. - Talk with them about it and answer all their questions.
. BE HONEST
(e.g. I had a ceiling fan that needed a wire replaced and a bent blade holder straightened. I placed a note to this effect along with the price asked. In talking with a man, along with it's good points, I

again mentioned it's problems, adding that I was sure that the fan could easily be fixed by someone who knew how. Instead of having to throw away the fan, I was $10 richer.)

When you are honest about an item you feel better, and customers are happy with their purchase. This is essential if you are planning to have other garage sales. People remember good and not so good experiences and talk about them.

NITTY GRITTY

This chapter deals with the actual physical work of preparing a sale.

COMFORT

Nothing makes a person feel tired all over like feet that ache.

It is important while preparing for and during a sale to wear COMFORTABLE SHOES with cushioning support in the soles. Many hours are spent standing and walking on the cement garage floor. Jogging shoes are ideal to wear because of their cushioned soles.

It is surprising how much longer you feel energetic when wearing appropriate shoes.

SECRETS OF PRICING

MARKING:

Use MASKING TAPE for price tags. You can quickly mark it and then tear the tape to put on an item. The following are some exceptions:

. Group signs are adequate for books or a box of small items.
. Larger signs are needed for mowers, bikes, tvs, and other large or special items.
. Paper with pins should be used on special or extra nice items. It is important not to put tape where it will leave a visible mark when removed.

When several people include items in the sale, it is necessary to identify each item. Use NAME INITIALS on each tag for ease of keeping track of who sold what.

Let the children help mark their items with price and their initials. Double check the prices. Smaller children have difficulty in understanding reasonable value. A $1 might seem like a lot to them for a relatively expensive item, or they could put $10 on an inexpensive item because they have enjoyed it so much. The children will be excited over the thought of making money for something they really don't want anymore.

WHAT PRICE TO PUT ON ITEMS:

It is desirable to price items in such a way that the return is fair to you, and the purchase price is fair to the customer. Often this seems to be one of the hardest things to determine. By using the following hints, it is really quite easy.

THINGS TO CONSIDER IN PRICING:
. ORIGINAL PRICE OF ITEM
> The most money to expect for top condition items is about 1/4 of the original price. Since most garage sale items look worn, the price can be much less especially with clothing. There are exceptions. See the following:

. AGE OF ITEM
> The newer the item - the bigger the price, unless an item is a collectable or an antique. See chapter on "Hidden Treasure

. CONDITION OF ITEM
> If item is new or like new (hardly worn or used), say "NEW" or "LIKE NEW" on the tag. Mark a higher price than you have on more worn items.

. MARKET FOR ITEM
> Popular items or "in" clothes, can be marked a little higher than average. (e.g. Levi Jeans compared with no name, RCA TV or brand X, baby crib).

. LARGER ITEMS
> More expensive items can bring as much as 1/3 of original value.

SECRET: CLEAN AND NEAT ITEMS WILL BRING TOP DOLLAR.

KEY QUESTION TO ASK YOURSELF: "If I WANTED this item, what is the MOST I WOULD BE WILLING TO PAY for it?". What you would pay; someone else would probably pay. Price items to ALLOW FOR BARGAINING, especially on larger items. Many people consider bargaining a tradition at garage sales.

BARGAINING

BEFORE THE SALE, DETERMINE the BOTTOM PRICE for which you will be willing to sell an item. That way you won't be caught off guard when someone makes an offer. (e.g. Bike for sale: predetermine $30 bottom price. Place price of $35 or $37 on bike, and hope for $32 or better.)

For those of you unfamiliar with bargaining, it goes something like this.
. You have a price listed - 37.00.
     (Note: no $ sign. See why below.)
. Customer offers 30.00.
. You say "Maybe 35.00".
. Customer accepts or offers 32.00.
. You say "I'll split the difference with you - 33.50".
With smaller amounts you might want to accept their first offer. e.g. 1.25 item, offer of 1.00.

SECRET: USE THE PSYCHOLOGY
OF PRICING AMOUNTS

Stores use pricing psychology all the time, and it can be incorporated into garage sales very easily. Even though there are only a few cents difference, people are much more willing to pay one price over another.

JUST UNDER THE WHOLE DOLLAR AMOUNT
An item will be bought much more quickly
for 1.95 than for 2 dollars.

ODD NUMBERS ENDINGS 5,7,9 INSTEAD OF EVEN
NUMBER ENDINGS 0,2,4,6,8
Odd numbers are more inviting than even numbers (e.g. 95¢ or 1.25 vs. 1.00, 25.00 or 27.00 vs. 20.00 or 30.00).

USE THE ¢ MARK BUT NOT THE $ MARK
(e.g. 45¢, 1.95, 15.00). Psychologically the $ mark makes people think the item is marked higher than what it is marked.

GO FOR THE STRETCH
For many items people will stretch a little and buy at an added 5, 15, 25, etc. cents over the price they might have preferred to pay. For larger items they will stretch an added 1-2 dollars.

Be sure to add that little extra when you are thinking about what price to put on an item.

ORGANIZATION

For people to buy, they must see the items and see them looking their best.

It is often too much trouble for customers to "root-through" a lot of items. So arrange everything to be easily seen.

GROUP ITEMS IN CATEGORIES

GENERAL - toys, jewelry, clothes, kitchen, tools, etc.

SPECIFIC - separate clothes into baby, boys, girls, children, teens, men, women. Make piles for small, medium, large.

Hang up clothing that you would normally find in a closet. Neatly fold other clothing. Make signs to show grouping and size.

SECRETS OF DISPLAY

How an item looks and where it is placed can help or hinder its sale.

LOOKS

All items should look clean and neat.

. Use a wet paper towel to wipe dusty items.
. Use the dishwasher to make glasses and dishes sparkle.
. Use the clothes dryer, adding a damp towel, to quickly remove wrinkles and freshen clothes. It only takes minutes.
. Use " elbow grease" on dirty and rusty items (e.g. an old refrigerator, mower, bike).

Looking good is especially important on higher priced items. The rewards of HIGHER DOLLAR RETURN are well worth a little bit of extra time spent.

33

PLACEMENT

Placement does make a difference if an item sells and for how much. (e.g. Who wants to look at and buy jewelry that is next to some rusty tools, or some drinking glasses next to old tennis shoes.) Just use your common sense and think how you would feel about an item when placing it in your garage sale. Be creative.

> **SECRET: IF AN ITEM DOES NOT SELL AT ONE PLACE, MOVE IT SOMEWHERE ELSE.**

This **MOVEMENT STRATEGY** can be especially helpful with larger more expensive items but is very effective with any item. I am not recommending mass movement of items, just minor moves here and there. (e.g. If a mower hasn't sold the 1st day on the right side of the driveway, put it on the left the next day. If a TV didn't sell on a cart, put it on a table. Switch the boys clothes with the girls clothes. Put toys on a different table.)

REORGANIZE

It is important to refold clothes and to keep all items in their proper areas. This can easily be done when there are no customers around. However, it can be beneficial to be working with one area while a customer is in another. This is showing that you care about the items, so they will too. Doing this while they are there also gives them a feeling of interaction rather than feeling "looked at" by someone just sitting.

BEING
PREPARED

MEALS

When having a garage sale, one of the biggest concerns is what to do about meals.

In the "Family Involvement" chapter there are suggestions for getting help from the family. Maybe there is a budding cook in the family. Now is a perfect opportunity for him/her to plan and organize a whole meal (with only a little input from you). If you don't have someone, that's ok. The family can at least help with setting the table, cleaning it off, and doing the dishes.

Ideally someone goes out and brings prepared food in. Since that is not practical for the entire time of the sale, here are some quick and easy recipes to help make meal times a whiz.

KEY: PLAN AHEAD WHAT YOU WILL DO
FOR EACH MEAL DURING THE SALE
AND HAVE ALL INGREDIENTS ON HAND.
KEEP MEALS SIMPLE.

Do think seriously about bringing in at least one meal
(whether it is pizza delivered, or someone going to pick
up chicken or hamburgers and fries).

The following recipes are written in a quick "read & do"
format.

MEXICAN CHICKEN   Prep time 10-15 min.

SAUTE   **2 Tbs butter (margarine)**
               1 green pepper
               1 medium onion, diced
USE large bowl
ADD and MIX with above ingredients:
               1 can Cream Chicken Soup
               1 can Cream Mushroom Soup
               2-3 cans Swanson chicken pieces (can
                    use 3 cups chicken pieces)
               1 can Rotel Tomatoes
               8 oz. Doritos (save some for top)
               1/2 lb cheddar cheese, grated
               1/2 cup water or chicken broth
PUT mixture in 3 qt. greased casserole.
ADD some Doritos and cheese on top.
BAKE 300°-350°   30-45 Min.   Serves 6-8

PORK STEAK-VEGETABLE BAKE   Prep 10-15 min.

COMBINE in sauce pan for stove or dish for microwave

    1 envelope onion soup mix
    1 cup water
    4 Tbs soy sauce

BRING to boil
PLACE in bottom of 9x13 baking dish:

    4-5 medium potatoes, peeled and cut
       lengthwise in 1/4 inch slices
    2 large carrots, sliced

SPOON 1/2 of mixture over potatoes and carrots
TOP WITH **4-8 pork steaks**.   Important to trim off fat.
       (optional: can brown in skillet be-
       fore adding)
SPOON remainder of soup mixture over meat.
BAKE COVERED 45-60 min. (UNCOVER last 10) 350°
Serves 4-6

FIVE CAN CASSEROLE   Prep 10 min.

MIX   **1 sm. can boneless chicken**
       1 can cream of mushroom soup
       1 can Chinese (chow mein)
         noodles
       1 can chicken with rice soup
       1 small can evaporated milk. I use less
         than a whole can.
       1 small onion, minced
       1/2 cup diced celery
       1/2 cup sliced almonds

MIX all ingredients. Put in baking dish.
Bake 350° 1 hr.

Note: Five Can Casserole can be started in a MW 20 min. on med. level (stirring several times) and finished for 10 to 15 min. in oven.

QUICK CHICKEN AND BISCUITS   Prep 10 min.

MIX   **2 cans cream of chicken soup.** A little
                 water can be added if desired.
             2 cans (5 oz.) boneless chicken
HEAT ingredients in oven, MW or on the stove.
PREPARE   **2-3 cans refrigerated biscuits**
SERVE cream chicken over biscuits.

Additional biscuits are delicious with butter and honey.
Cooking time 15 min.   Serves 5-6

OVEN BURGERS   Prep 10 min.

COMBINE   **3/4 cup soft bread crumbs** (1 slice),
             **1/2 can condensed Cheddar cheese
                 soup,(total 2 cans)**
             1 Tbs. dried minced onions (or sm. reg.
                 onion, diced),
             1/2 tsp salt.
Add   **1 1/2 lbs. lean ground beef** and mix well.
                 Shape into 6 patties. Place in bak-
                 ing dish.

38

BLEND together **1 1/2 cans Cheddar Cheese soup,**
  2/3 cup chili sauce,
  3 Tbs prepared mustard.
POUR 1/2 of mixture over patties. Set remainder aside.
BAKE covered about 30 minutes.
SPOON or pour off any excess grease. Pour on remain-
  ing soup mixture.
BAKE uncovered about 15 minutes more or until done.
COOK regular **noodles**.
Serve patties over hot cooked noodles.
Bake 350°   Approx. 45 min.   Serves 6

HOT HAM SANDWICHES   Prep 5 min.

PLACE   **Shredded or chipped ham**
ON   **Hamburger buns**
ADD   **Cheese of your choice**
WRAP each separately in foil
PLACE in oven immediately or keep in refrigerator for
          later. Can be used one at a time or all at
          once.
BAKE 350°   about 20 min.

FOR MICROWAVE - individual: on small plate place ham
with cheese on top. MW med. until hot. Slide onto bun.
Larger number: can use a larger plate with a number of
mounds of ham and cheese to MW all at one time.
    Many children like to do this with bologna.

TUNA BURGERS
Prep 10 -15 min.

COMBINE - MIX   **1 can tuna**, drained
1/4 cup celery, finely chopped
1/2 cup grated cheddar cheese
1/2 sm. onion, finely chopped
1/3 cup mayonnaise
PUT INTO   **Hamburger buns**
WRAP in foil as above and bake.
350°   about 20 min.

TACO SALAD SMORGASBORD
Prep 20 min.

BROWN   **1 lb. hamburger** (can cook in MW)
OPTIONAL: ADD **1 pkg. taco seasoning** and water per package directions.
OR USE **taco or picante sauce** on top of assembled salad
PUT hamburger mixture in dish
PREPARE AHEAD other dishes of
   onions, chopped
   tomatoes, chopped
   cheddar cheese, shredded
   1 can kidney beans, drained
   Large bowl of **lettuce**, shredded
   Dorito or tortilla chips, crushed (can use a plastic bag for easy no mess crushing)

Let everyone assemble their own taco salad with desired ingredients.
Serves 4 with 1 lb. of hamburger

40

ICE BOX DESERT   Prep 15 min.

CRUSH   **1 1/4 cup vanilla wafers**
PUT IN buttered 9x13 pan.
CREAM   **1/2 cup butter**
                  1 1/2 cups sifted powdered sugar
ADD   **2 EGGS** one at a time
MIX THOROUGHLY POUR OVER WAFERS
ARRANGE ON TOP **4 cups sliced fresh**
                  peaches or strawberries
TOP WITH   **1 cup cool whip**
SPREAD TO EDGE TO SEAL
SPRINKLE SOME EXTRA CRUMBS ON TOP
CHILL overnight   Serves 10-12

EASY DUMP CAKE   Prep 10 min.

Into 9x13 baking pan
DUMP   **1 can (20 oz) crushed pineapple** with
                  juice
SPREAD evenly
DUMP   **1 can cherry pie filling**
SPREAD evenly over pineapple
SPRINKLE   **1 package yellow cake** mix evenly over
                  fruit
DISTRIBUTE **1 1/2 sticks butter** evenly over top (slice
                  very thin)
SPREAD **nuts** over top (Optional)

BAKE 350°   30-35 min.   Serves 8-10

41

SUGGESTION: For ease, use paper plates as often as possible for meals.

QUICK AND EASY MISCELLANEOUS SUGGESTIONS:

RICE KRISPY BARS (Recipe on box)
> This is really quick when done in the Microwave and using miniature marshmallows. Cocoa Krispies can be used along with peanut butter.

FROZEN JUICE - Can be frozen in ice cube trays and then crushed. Frozen in small paper cups, it can be eaten by tearing some of the upper part of the cup away.

ICE CREAM CONES - sugar cones can be an added treat.

CHILDREN'S ACTIVITIES

The next biggest concern we have during a garage sale is how to take care of and occupy the kids, especially young ones.

Older children can be very helpful with the other children, or with the sale itself.

Here are some simple activities that can be used.

ACTIVITY: **PAINTING THE OUTSIDE OF THE HOUSE OR DRAWING ON THE SIDEWALK**. Kids love it.

NEEDED: **Old paint brush** (big)

Bucket or pan of **water**.

Guide lines of do's and don'ts

ACTIVITY: **DRAWING ON THE SIDEWALK**

NEEDED: **Chalk** - variety of colors makes this lots of fun. (The chalk can be hosed off afterward or left for the rain to do the job).

ACTIVITY: **TARGET SHOOTING**

NEEDED: **String**

Aluminum pans (small & large)

Squirt guns or old spray bottles

The pans can swing from tree limbs, swing sets, or even be attached to the children. The noise announces a hit. Specific moving targets are lots of fun. They are more of a challenge than a stationary target and less bothersome than having everything as targets. Trash can lids make effective shields for a water battle.

ACTIVITY: **RUNNING THROUGH THE SPRINKLER**

This is always a winner.

ACTIVITY: **A NEW TOY, GAME, OR BOOK**

NEEDED: **A trip to a garage sale**

43

Go to some garage sales several weeks before yours. Buy some games or toys that will be new to your children. If they go along to choose, make sure they understand that they must WAIT to play with the games until the family sale. Take the items home and <u>you</u> hide them or put them away. Don't let the children keep them. The games need to seem fresh and new to them on sale day.

ACTIVITY: **HAVE A SPECIAL FRIEND OVER OR GO TO THEIR HOUSE**

ACTIVITY: **WRITE LETTERS OR DRAW PICTURES FOR GRANDPARENTS**
Subject: the garage sale or anything else
NEEDED: **Plain paper**
Pen or pencil
Colored markers or crayons

If the children choose to just write, suggest that they decorate the stationery.

ACTIVITY: **STILT CANS**
NEEDED: **2 cans for each child** - large juice cans or tuna cans for small children. (Fatter bean cans can also be used for in-between size stilts. Soup cans, regular vegetable cans, and other small diameter cans are

unsuitable, because their footing is not stable enough).

Clothes line rope (strong so it can not break - large so it is gentle on the hands)

Large nail & hammer

1 - Cut the tops off cans (leave bottoms on).
2 - Turn cans over (bottom ends up).
3 - With nail, punch a hole on each side of the cans about an inch or less down from the new top (less with smaller cans).
4 - From the outside of the can, put one end of the rope through a hole and tie a big knot on the inside. This is to prevent the rope from coming loose.
5 - Take the other end of rope and do the same in the other hole.

It is important to fit the rope length to the child. The rope should fit comfortably in a child's hands (as he stands on the cans) with his arms hanging down in front of him.

The key to be able to use the stilts well is to keep pulling on the ropes (to keep them tight against the feet) while standing or walking.

This is great fun for outside only. Used inside the cans can cause marks on the floor.

ACTIVITY: **BALLOONS**
Balloons can be a lot of fun used in a variety of ways.

Volley balloon - a string can be put up as a net to play volley balloon by batting balloon over the net.

Filled with water - for throwing.

ACTIVITY: **BUBBLES**

NEEDED: **Bubble soap and wand**

If you have an old wand around the house, you can make your own inexpensive soap formula for hours of fun.

FORMULA: 1/8 cup Dish washing Soap (Dawn works well)

1 cup water (mix well)

If your particular brand of soap does not work well, try adding a Tbs of glycerin (bought at discount or drug store). This sometimes helps the bubble last longer.

ACTIVITY: **PARACHUTING**

NEEDED: **15x15 (approx) piece of material or a large handkerchief**

String (4 - 14 inch pieces)

Object to tie on

1 - Tie a string to each corner of the material.
2 - Tie other ends of string to object.
3 - Start wrapping string LOOSELY around object. Continue wrapping until string and parachute are both wrapped around object.

4 - Throw underhand high into the air.
Parachute will open and object float to the ground.

For lower throws hold just the tip of parachute (with string and object dangling) and throw underhand up into the air.

ACTIVITY: **CHILDREN'S PICNIC LUNCH**
Let the children help plan what to have and make the sandwiches or what ever. Be sure to have picnic food on hand. (Plan before going to the grocery). A blanket can be used under a shade tree, a small play table and chairs can be brought outside, or TV trays and lawn chairs can be used. Be sure to use paper plates to make it special. Let them serve you.

ACTIVITY: **NEW THINGS TO DO**
NEEDED: **A visit to the library**
The library is a FANTASTIC SOURCE of all kinds of exciting reading, game, and activity books.

Plan a visit to the library a couple days before the sale. Help the children find books for activities which they can handle without much help or supervision.
Sample Coin Trick found in library book:
Hold the arm straight out with palm down.
Bend arm at the elbow so hand comes back over the shoulder (palm is now up). Place 2 pennies on the forearm near the elbow.
Quickly swing arm down and try to catch

the pennies without them falling to the floor. More and more pennies can be added. It is exciting to see who can catch the most pennies.

ACTIVITY: **FRISBEE GOLF**
    NEEDED: **A frisbee for each person**
    GOAL: See who can hit a target in the fewest number of throws. (Take turns as in golf).
    TARGET WINNER: Person with the least number of throws to hit target.
    GAME WINNER: Person with the most targets won.

Pick out targets one at a time as you go along or all of them before starting the game. (e.g. trees, swing set, sand box, bush, telephone pole, picnic table).

WEATHER

To be comfortable during your sale, have a fan or heater (whichever is needed) ready to use. This will benefit you and make your customers more comfortable, thus in a BETTER FRAME OF MIND TO LOOK AND BUY.

Note: TURN GARAGE LIGHTS ON. Most garages look more cheery and have better visibility with lights, especially if the day is overcast. Consider using your lighting no matter what the weather.

RECORD KEEPING

Record keeping is important but can be VERY SIMPLE. All you need is a sheet of paper or NOTEBOOK.

DIVIDE the paper into separate areas for each person with items in the sale, or have an individual sheet for each one. WRITE down the total of each sale under the correct name.

It is really not necessary to keep records if you are the only one in the sale. However, I suggest a record no matter how many there are. It is fun to see the list of sales accumulating and to total them.

CHANGE

$40 should give you adequate change so there is no need to panic. If possible, have a few extra one dollar bills in the house in case you get a couple of $20's early in the sale. People are usually very considerate and try to give you right change, or at least small bills.

A good mix is
$28	in	1's
$ 5	in	quarters
$ 5	in	dimes
$ 2	in	nickels

START EARLY

Starting early to prepare for your sale is important. It saves late night hours and a lot of hassles. You and your family will enjoy a smooth running sale when STARTING EARLY, PLANNING AHEAD, and BEING PREPARED.

Give yourself at least 3 weeks if possible. That doesn't mean that you will be busy with garage sale things for a solid 3 weeks. It means you'll be getting yourself and family in gear for the sale.

To get a head start, you can keep "garage sale" in mind all year long. Put things aside as you find them. Have a special bag or boxes to put items in as you decide you don't need them any longer. It is satisfying to reduce clutter so quickly this way.

SAFEGUARDS

. IF YOU GO INTO THE HOUSE - Take the money with
  you

. DON'T KEEP LARGE AMOUNT OF MONEY OUTSIDE
  EVEN WHEN YOU ARE THERE. Take extra
  money inside. Hide it somewhere. Note: The full
  amount of money will be needed outside the first
  morning. Later in the day and the next days, less
  money will be necessary outside for change. You
  can always go inside to get change if needed.

. BE CAREFUL that no one follows you inside unin-
  vited.

. BE CAUTIOUS about letting someone use your phone.
  Perhaps you can make the call for them.

. IF ANYONE NEEDS TO USE THE BATHROOM, be
  sure to watch to see that they go into the bathroom and nowhere else. They could take something or "case" the house.

. WHILE YOU ARE GOING TO BE IN THE GARAGE, lock all other outside doors and window.
. IF YOU ARE ALONE, leave a radio or TV on inside the house so others will be convinced that you are not alone. You can even go in and pretend to talk with your family if you feel it would be helpful.

This is not written to make anyone fearful, but as wise counsel for your protection.

I must be quick to mention that all the garage sale customers I've had over the years have been pleasant people and honest.

REAL

TREASURE

TREASURE HUNTING

Items don't have to be old, rare, or expensive to bring unexpected cash into your pockets. There is a whole WORLD OF COLLECTORS just waiting to hear about your "find" and to pay you lots of money for it.

Many valuable items are unknowingly sold at garage sales (at garage sale prices) or thrown away as junk.

> (e.g. A $2,500 tin can sold at a yard sale for $12. A Los Angeles family threw out $500,000 worth of old letters because they did not think they were important.)

Most items do not have tremendous value, but many do have much greater value than what we might think.

This subject is far to vast for much to be said in this book. My purpose for including this chapter is to make you aware of the possibility of treasure in your possession and to encourage you to find out what to do with it.

Take time to FIND OUT WHAT YOU HAVE.
Take time to CHECK PRICES.
Take time to FIND THE RIGHT BUYER.

WHEN FINDING AN ITEM OF VALUE THE KEY TO GETTING TOP DOLLAR IS REACH-ING THE BEST BUYER.

BUYERS

You have two choices: either take an item to a local dealer or try to sell it yourself.

Remember, a dealer buys to resell. He will give you about half of what the item is worth but will save you the time and effort of finding another buyer.

Locating your own buyer is more profitable, especially with rare finds.

Once you know what to look for and how to locate high dollar buyers, you can be on a continuous treasure hunt wherever you go. Who knows what you will find to sell?

THE KEY TO MAXIMUM PROFIT IS TO FIND BUYERS THAT ARE COLLECTORS.

There are many national expert collectors that will gladly help you discover the value of a particular item and buy it from you. Many will also help you find another buyer if they are not interested at the moment.

In seeking free information be sure to include a long #10 self addressed stamped envelope. This shows that you are truly interested in an answer. It also shows consideration for the potential buyer.

It is not difficult to dispose of items over the phone and by mail. There are books that tell you how. One of them is "Cash for Your Undiscovered Treasures" by Dr. H. Hyman.

Here are just a few tips:
. FIND A SOURCE (see below)
. CONTACT THE SOURCE by letter.
. LET THEM KNOW you are an amateur seller trying to find the item's value. Ask them to make an offer and give helpful suggestions.
. INCLUDE a detailed description of the item and possibly a photo or copy of it. It is possible to photo copy many items including plates. Be sure to state its condition (listing any cracks, chips, missing pages, etc.)
. NEVER SEND THE ITEM without satisfactory prior arrangements.
. REMEMBER to include a long SASE (self addressed stamped envelope).

**THE KEY IS FINDING REPUTABLE COL-
LECTORS. THERE ARE MANY OF THEM.**

CAUTION: If an item is of great value, be sure to check the credentials and references of the collector before sending the item. Also, find out how to arrange the transfer of the item so you are protected against loss, theft, or breakage.

SOURCES OF INFORMATION

The best source of information is your local library. A second source is knowledgeable local dealers. Many times they have books available for you to see.

At the library, look in the CARD FILE for ANTIQUES and for COLLECTIBLES.

Here are a few of the BOOKS I found when looking:
"Time Life Encyclopedia of Collectibles"
"Kovel's Antiques & Collectibles Price List"
"Official 1988 Price Guide to Collector Plates"
"Warman's Antiques & Their Prices" (It has pictures.)

There is a MAGAZINE named "The Antique Trader Price Guide to Antiques and Collectors' Items". This has prices and pictures. A special yearly price guide with 912 pages and 1500 photos is also available.

A good source for getting more information is an ENCYCLOPEDIA OF ASSOCIATIONS. It has ADDRESSES of individuals, specialists, and clubs interested in collectibles.

Looking at ADS IN PERIODICALS for specific offers to buy is another way of finding collectors.

OLD TREASURE

How old is old? If an item is over 15 years old, there is potential that there is a collector somewhere willing to pay cash for it.

Five of the most valuable baseball cards date from the 50's. Miss Revlon, Tressy, Barbie Dolls, and GI Joes are in demand. Old TV Guides (some from as late at '82 bring 3-4.00).

THERE IS A MARKET FOR:
Spark plugs, sheet music, items showing people's hands, cookbooks, buttons, True Detective Magazines (70's and back), marbles, glassware, bottles, Disney items, Coca Cola advertising items, graniteware, knives, paper dolls, comic books, McDonald's Uniforms, advertising literature for Chevrolet Corvette (1953-80), boy scout items, license plates, wooden nickels from Missouri & Colorado, neon signs, advertising pocket mirrors, Pearl Harbor items, dog

and cat license tags before 1950, toy tractors, music boxes, and thousands more items.

IT IS AMAZING WHAT PEOPLE COLLECT.

FUTURE TREASURE

What will collectors be looking for in the future? Charles Jordan has written a book "What to Save from the '80's: A Guide for Collectors".

The point is - choose carefully the items you keep and those you do not.

Guessing tomorrow's collectable is about 25% chance and 75% knowing how to evaluate an item's potential.

Many collectibles are things from childhood years or a specific era of the past. Others are linked to major events, people and places.

Some potential future collectibles are:
original signed cabbage patch dolls plus accessories, items linked with major advertisers' promotions, items from major public events like political races and the restructure of the Statue of Liberty (e.g. a chip of stone from the base of the original Statue), Pee Wee Herman dolls, an empty bottle of Paul Newman's own salad dressing, video games of the '70's especially pac man and linked items (cereal boxes, etc.). There are, however, no guarantees.

Keep in mind that only about 1 in 10 of the items marketed specifically as collectibles will go up in value.

If you want to guess and take a chance, remember the CONDITION of an object affects its worth along with the SUPPLY of items on the market.

HAPPY TREASURE HUNTING !

HELPFUL

HINTS

VISIT OTHER GARAGE SALES   especially if you have never been to many before. Learn what you like and don't like about them. See which you enjoy going to and which you don't. Ask yourself "why?". Use this information to make your sale even better. Keep your eyes open for Treasure.

ENCOURAGE OTHERS IN YOUR NEIGHBORHOOD to have their SALES AT THE SAME TIME as yours. I know of whole allotments that schedule a time for garage sales every year for those desiring to participate. A choice of so many items all in one area is a powerful drawing card. Extra big bucks can be made.

EVEN ONE SALE ACROSS THE STREET can be of help to bring more people to your sale.

AD WORDS

DON'T SAY "ANNUAL" (even if it is). This says there is only a years worth of items for sale.

DO SAY "ESTATE" (if it is). This says there is an extra large selection of items and possibly some antiques and collectibles.

DO SAY "MOVING" (if you are). This says that there lots of good buys.

SPECIFIC - NOT TOO SPECIFIC IN ADS

When listing specific items in your ad, don't be too specific. (e.g. list sofa, not beige sofa. Reason: With sofa, ALL THE PEOPLE interested in a sofa will come see. If a color is mentioned, people wanting a grey sofa won't bother to come.)

AD WORDS TO OMIT TO SAVE MONEY

Garage - The ad is already listed under the Garage Sale Column.

Town - This can be omitted as long as sale is local.

State and Phone - No need to list these.

BE READY FOR LOTS OF CLUTTER DURING PREPARATION TIME, BUT DON'T BE OVERWHELMED BY THE MESS. It is ok and will all get straightened out more easily than you think.

USE ¢ MARK BUT NOT $ sign when pricing (e.g. 45¢, 1.75 and 25.-). People respond better without a visible $ sign.

PRICE THEN ORGANIZE - Have a special area to put items as they are priced. Keep them separate from the unpriced items. This saves a lot of confusion. Organize for display later.

INCLUDE small things (really anything) even though it doesn't appear to have much value (shells picked up on vacation, pieces of yarn, odd parts to anything). People often buy items to be used for something other than what they were originally designed. It always feels great when someone says "That is just what I've been looking for. I'm going to use it for _____."

HANGING CLOTHING - It is not always easy to find a way to hang items in the yard or garage. The best advice I have is to be creative. A caution: be sure that everything is stable so nothing will accidentally fall on a customer.

LAST DAY ADDITIONS - have your friends wait until A DAY OR TWO BEFORE the sale to bring their items. You will already be organized so this will not add to your mess. A key ingredient for this to go smoothly is for them to have their ARTICLES ALREADY PRICED. This really saves time, effort and frayed emotions.

SCHEDULE YOUR HELP - Some extra help is nice to have when opening on the 1st day. Be sure, however, that not everyone comes then. It is nice to have help a couple hours close to meal times and on other days.

Have your SIGNS READY AND UP the night before or very early in the morning - an hour ahead is timely.

Be sure there are SIGNS AT EVERY TURN GETTING TO YOUR HOUSE. Other people do not know your allotment or country road. I have been frustrated many times trying to find a sale and have had to give up before finding it.
MAKE IT EASY TO FIND YOU.

If you like COFFEE in the mornings, have it perked and your cup filled before opening for business.

HAVE AN EXTENSION CORD READY to allow customers to test electrical items.

EARLY BIRDS - EXPECT THEM. WHO ARE THEY?
1 - People who want to be sure to get a look at a particular item advertised.
2 - People who have put your sale first on their list.

63

3 - Collectors and Dealers (These are people who buy
      items to resell).

Many times "early birds" will be peering in your garage
windows or waiting in cars outside long before you
planned to open. DON'T BE INTIMIDATED OR RUSHED
WHEN YOU ARE NOT READY. It can be very frustrating
and emotionally draining if you get off to a running start
before you're ready.   When the day starts rushed, you
can be feeling tired by 11. Often "early birds" will rush
in, take a quick look, and rush right back out, or offer
you a very low price on an item.

When you follow the checklist in the next chapter you'll
be ready to open extra early (if you like).

OFF SITE ITEMS - boat, motorcycle, piano, etc. Display
a sign or even a picture and mention the item to your
customers.   Say "Do you know anyone interested in a
boat? We have one for sale." If they show in-terest, tell
them about it and show them a picture. Take NAMES
AND PHONE NUMBERS FOR THE OWNER to call OR
give the person the OWNERS NUMBER.

DON'T BE CAUGHT OFF GUARD:
DECIDE AHEAD OF TIME the BOTTOM PRICE for which
you will sell the item. People will bargain with you at a
sale. Always allow for that in the original pricing. How
eager you are to sell a certain item will help determine
your pricing and how far down you will bargain.

DECIDE AHEAD OF TIME whether or not you are willing to TAKE CHECKS and what your criteria will be. How large a check are you willing to take? Will you take local and/or out-of-town checks?

Be sure to be extra cautious when thinking about taking a check for a large amount. If there is a bank close ask them if they would mind taking their check to the bank and bring back cash. I did this one time, and the person did not mind. I have never had a check from a garage sale customer bounce. Feel free to ask for drivers license and credit card info and write it on the check.

———————

DON'T BE QUICK TO TAKE LESS FOR AN ITEM, especially on the 1st day. The person is definitely interested in the article or would not have made an offer. I have always had the policy that I don't take less on large items on the first day of a sale. I very nicely tell the customer that. Often they will buy anyway. If not, I take their name and phone number and call them later or give them my number for them to check back with me. Many times the item is sold when they do call back.

Dealers will, many times, make a low offer. Usually you have the item priced right. They want to get it for less so they can resell it at a profit.

———————

FOR SALES EFFECT - a cassette player, TV, or radio for sale can be playing.

———————

WHAT TO EXPECT:

1st day x $	Swamped at opening or before & steady flow of customers
2nd day 1/2 x $	Occasional customers, slower starting day
3rd day 1/4 x $	Most people are not up and out very early on Saturdays. Children and husband are home. Opening a little later is fine.

EXTRAS - If your neighborhood has a lot of children, you might have some of them just hanging around. They might want to watch what is going on or to keep looking and looking at the sale items, especially toys and games. Feel free to ask them to leave once they have looked. Your other customers need full access to your sale.

IT IS NOT NECESSARY to be tied to the sale all the time. If there are no customers, take the money and go into the house if you like. BE SURE TO WATCH AND LISTEN so when customers do come, you can be there to greet them as they approach.

SLOW TIMES - Be alert. Often larger items are sold during slow times.

STAYING OPEN LONGER HOURS THAN STATED IN NEWSPAPER AD - People will wander in as long as the signs are still up. Closing at the stated hours is fine. If it is convenient, staying open longer hours is no burden. Most of the time can be spent in the house with need to come out only on occasion. Since the hardest work is done, this is an additional way to make a few extra dollars.

———————

BE SLOW TO MARK EVERYTHING DOWN THE LAST DAY. If you are planning to have sales other years, don't mark it down. People will remember this and wait until the last day to come or ask for lower prices even on the 1st day. If this will be your only sale and you really want everything gone, then mark it down.

———————

CRAFTS YOU MAKE can be a profitable addition in the garage sale. It is helpful if business cards or fliers are available for possible future sales.

CHECKLIST

FOR

SUCCESS

Having read this book, you are well on your way to having an OUTSTANDING, BIG DOLLAR SALE. By following the CHECKLIST below, your sale can be smooth running (free from time pressures and unexpected surprises).

GETTING STARTED:

____ Let your family in on the good news about the sale

____ Begin immediately collecting sale items even if not going to have the sale for awhile. (e.g. next spring)

DECISIONS:

Dates of sale _____

Day 1 _____ Time _____

Day 2 _____ Time _____

Day 3 _____ Time _____

OTHERS TAKING PART - CAN CAN'T

_____ ____ ____

_____ ____ ____

_____ ____ ____

_____ ____ ____

_____ ____ ____

_____ ____ ____

ALLOW TIME TO GET READY - SO NOT RUSHED AND HASSLED

3 WEEKS AHEAD (INCLUDES 3 WEEKENDS)
___ Clean the garage
___ Remind friends of sale dates if planned awhile back
___ Begin going through your entire house (closets, draw-ers, storage areas). Evaluate everything. Is this something for the garage sale?
___ Build family enthusiasm for the sale

2 WEEKS AHEAD (INCLUDES 2 WEEKENDS)
___ Set up table for displays
___ Fix way to hang clothing
___ Cover unsightly garage areas and valuable items
___ Get serious about going through closets, drawers, etc. for sale items

___ Keep eyes open for Treasure
___ Help children go through teirr items if needed
___ Begin cleaning more difficult itmes
___ Start washing extra dishes and soiled clothes with your regular washing or even do special loads to clean and freshen
___ Call newspaper to find out conditions for placing ads and deadline (Make notes on checklist if different from those indicated by *)

1 WEEK AHEAD (INCLUDES 1 WEEKEND)
___ Start pricing (this should be almost completed by 2-3 days before sale)
___ Do general organizing
___ Continue collecting items
___ Continue cleaning itmes
___ Continue to involve family

3 DAYS AHEAD
___ Arramge for friends to bring their items. (The day before the sale is the best time for this.) Be sure most of your items are already priced and organized.
___ Check to see how much more table space will be needed - perhaps they can bring some tables
___ Gather information to include in ad *
___ Write ad *
___ Do signs or arrange to have them done by family
___ CONTINUE PRICING & ORGANIZING

2 DAYS AHEAD

___ Plan meals
___ Take of call ad to newspaper *
___ Grocery shop
___ Get change at bank
___ Do other needful errands
___ Schedule people to help at sale
___ See that signs are completed

DAY BEFORE

___ Finish pricing
___ Finish organizing & display
___ Make food
___ Get fan or heater if weather requires

EVENING BEFORE

___ Set up table as a desk
___ Have sale ready to go
Set out
___ . Change in container
___ . Record book
___ . Calculator
___ . Pen & masking tape
___ . Yardstick
___ Have signs up or ready for morning

MORNING OF SALE

___ Put signs up at least an hour ahead
___ Have self ready to start 1/2 hour early
___ Straighten kitchen
___ Take out items set out last night
___ Take out cup of coffee

DAY OF SALE

___ Smile a lot and be friendly
___ Be helpful and available
___ Be cautious
___ Work with sale items -
    Rearrange them as they get messy
    Move items to a new location if not selling
        where they are
___ Enjoy yourself

END OF SALE

___ Count your profits
___ Divide money among participants - Be sure to take
        out for ad costs.
___ Take signs down
___ Evaluate sale
___ Decide what to keep - what not to keep
___ Prepare for next sale

NEXT TIME

Start now to plan for next year's sale. Cleaning up for this year and planning for next is simple.

3 CHOICES TO MAKE:
Look at each left over item and make a decision.
      1 - THROW IT AWAY
      2 - GIVE IT AWAY
      3 - STORE IT AWAY

THROW IT AWAY - This is easy.

GIVE IT AWAY - There are many worthwhile organizations that make good use of any item in reasonably good condition.

Put items <u>neatly</u> <u>in</u> <u>boxes</u> <u>or</u> <u>bags</u> and IMMEDIATELY put them in your car. It is too easy to allow these items to just sit in the garage waiting for a convenient time to take them some-place. The time to take them is the next time you go somewhere in the car.

STORE IT AWAY - Some items are ideal to keep for your next sale.

Most items can be stored with the price tags left on. Next year all you have to do is take items out of the box, and put them on the table. If clothes are packed carefully and neatly, often they are wrinkle-free enough to need no additional attention.

All of this takes JUST A LITTLE TIME.

PICK UP OF OTHER'S ITEMS
Encourage your friends to pick up their items as soon a possible. The following Monday should be the latest.

PUT AWAY THE SALES TABLES AND YOU ARE FINISHED. THERE IS THE BONUS OF HAVING A CLEAN GARAGE.

TAKE A FEW MINUTES to think about your sale. Make a note in your record book of anything you would like to do differently next time.

For an EVEN EASIER TIME NEXT YEAR, begin putting aside unused items as you find them.

EACH SALE YOU HAVE GETS EASIER AND MORE ENJOYABLE.

GARAGE
SALE

INDEX

HOW TO GET MORE CASH

	Chapter
Right timing	1
Best number of days	1
Maximize hours	1,9
How to get more items in the sale	1
Value of area sales	9
Developing a buy atmosphere	4
Getting more people to the sale	4
Winning classified ads	4
Signs that attract customers	4
Good placement of signs	4
Posters that draw people	4
Attitude toward items & people	2,4
Young entrepreneurs	3
Garage layout that attracts	4
Personal contact that sells	4
Secrets of Pricing	5
Using pricing psychology	5
Going for the stretch	5
Thoughtful placement of each item	5
Groupings and display	5
Using movement strategy	5
Predetermining bottom pricing	9
Preparing to bargain	5,9
Garage and yard attractiveness	5
Use of lighting	6
Salesmanship secrets	4
Hunting for hidden treasure	8
Getting high $ amount for your treasure	8
Adding craft items	9

HOW TO HAVE LESS HASSLE

Feeling confident and prepared to handle situations is the KEY TO BREEZING THROUGH A SALE.

	Chapter
Decisions getting started	1
Fitting your schedule	1
Convenient hours	1
Outside Help	1
Attitude toward sale	2
Getting family cooperation, interest	3
Knowing ways family can help	3
Your comfort	5
Easy pricing guidelines	5
Peace of mind	
Quick easy meals	6
Kids' Activities	6
Record keeping & change	6
Safeguards	7
Helpful hints	9
Checklist for success	10